# Jam Session

# *Barry Sanders*

## Terri Dougherty
### ABDO Publishing Company

## visit us at
## www.abdopub.com

Published by ABDO Publishing Company, 4940 Viking Drive, Suite 622, Edina, Minnesota 55435.
Copyright © 1999 by Abdo Consulting Group, Inc. International copyrights reserved in all countries.
No part of this book may be reproduced in any form without written permission from the publisher.

Printed in the United States.

Cover and Interior Photo credits: AP/Wide World Photos

Edited by Denis Dougherty

Sources: Detroit Free Press; Knight-Ridder News; The Sporting News; Sports Illustrated; Sports Illustrated For Kids; USA Today

### Library of Congress Cataloging-in-Publication Data

Dougherty, Terri.
    Barry Sanders / Terri Dougherty.
       p. cm. -- (Jam Session)
  Includes index.
  Summary: Examines the personal life and football career of the popular running back for the Detroit Lions.
  ISBN 1-57765-037-9 (hardcover)
  ISBN 1-57765-339-4 (paperback)
  1. Sanders, Barry, 1968 --Juvenile literature. 2. Football players--United States--Biography--Juvenile literature. 3. Detroit Lions (Football team)--Juvenile literature. [1. Sanders, Barry, 1968— 2. Football players. 3. Afro-Americans--Biography.]
  I. Title II. Series.
  GV939.S18D68  1999
  796.332'092--dc21
   [b]
                                              98-7744
                                                 CIP
                                                     AC

# Contents

# Lion King

*I*t was the final game of the 1997 season. The Detroit Lions needed a win over the New York Jets to make the playoffs. The Lions' hopes were riding on the powerful legs of running back Barry Sanders.

Barry is a nice guy who gives his opponents nightmares. But after nearly three quarters against the Jets, Barry didn't look like a dazzling runner who left tacklers grabbing at air. He had rushed for only 23 yards.

Then, on the last play of the third quarter, Barry broke loose. Slipping past defenders, he gained 47 yards!

Four plays later he took a handoff from quarterback Scott Mitchell, burst through a hole and zoomed into the end zone for a touchdown. His 15-yard run gave the Lions a 13-10 lead!

But that wasn't his high point of the game. On a two-yard gain with two minutes, 10 seconds to play, he joined an elite club: He became the third NFL player to rush for 2,000 yards in a season.

After Barry reached 2,000, the Pontiac Silverdome crowd went wild. He was mobbed by his teammates. Coach Bobby Ross wanted to send in another player to make sure Barry wouldn't lose yards.

But Barry refused. The team needed a crucial first down. He delivered with a 53-yard run to the Jets' three-yard line, and the Lions won 13-10. Barry finished with 2,053 yards, the second-highest season rushing total in NFL history! It was a great achievement, but Barry didn't brag.

"I'm just very, very lucky that I'm the one carrying the ball with the group," he said after the game. "I'm so fortunate that I've been able to stay healthy and do what I do, and be on the team that I'm on."

Barry Sanders (20), is carried off the field after he finished the game with 184 yards and more than 2,000 yards for the season.

# *Little Barry*

**B**arry bounces off tacklers, cuts through defenders, zips through invisible openings and keeps on going.

"I move more quickly than other backs. I use my speed and my agility to help me keep my balance," Barry said.

"There's no secret," he added. "I work hard, stay in shape, and lift weights. I work on the stuff that I can control." Although Barry makes it sound simple, he baffles defenders.

"He doesn't get touched on a lot of his runs," said Tony Dungy, head coach of the Tampa Bay Buccaneers. "You can't coach it. You can't practice against it because you don't know where he's going – and he probably doesn't know where he's going when the play starts."

"He has the most unusual ability to stop and start that I've ever seen," adds Dan Henning, former offensive coordinator at Detroit.

Barry's attitude makes him just as special as his running ability does. He's the best running back in the game, but others aren't jealous because he's so humble.

Barry credits his family when he's applauded for his character. "I had eight sisters and two brothers and grew up in a normal little neighborhood in Kansas," said Barry. "I got enough attention from my parents and friends and loved ones. I didn't have a deep craving to be some superstar or whatever."

Barry was born on July 16, 1968, the seventh of 11 children. The family lived in a three-bedroom home in Wichita, Kansas.

"It was never quiet," Barry remembers. "To have some privacy, I would go out and play basketball or go to a friend's house. I also had to share everything. For example, if I brought home a bag of potato chips, everybody had to have some. But I liked having a big family. Now, I get to share my success with a lot of people who care about me."

Barry's mother, Shirley, made sure the children went to church every Sunday. Barry's father, William, owned a roofing business.

"My parents are go-do-your-job people," Barry said. "They don't want anything from anybody. They want to take care of their own. I think that's exactly my approach to football. I'm not necessarily looking for fame and fortune. I try to make sure I uphold my end. I take care of business and go home."

Barry had to get good grades in school to play sports. His junior high football and basketball teams won city championships. He was happy, but winning didn't mean everything to him.

"I wasn't excessively competitive—I don't think my folks would have allowed it," he said. "They stressed other things besides winning. Life always was about more than that. I had to be a

good person. When I lost, I had to shake the other guy's hand."
He learned about football by watching players like Terry Metcalf
and Marcus Allen.

"I probably picked up a lot of things from those great runners,"
Barry once said. "Being small, I knew I had to be a creative,
innovative runner—not your typical straight-ahead runner."

When he was young, Barry didn't look like he'd become a great
athlete. He could run fast and change direction quickly, but didn't

grow as fast as other kids. In ninth grade he weighed barely 100 pounds and was five feet tall. His seventh-grade sister was taller!

"It was like, 'When am I going to grow?' " he said. Barry couldn't do anything about his height, but he could get stronger. When he was in high school, he lifted weights and his legs became exceptionally powerful.

"I have always admired small running backs," Barry said. "When I was a kid, I liked Tony Dorsett. Watching him gave me the confidence that I could play football and didn't have to be very big."

Opposite page: 1988 Heisman Trophy winner Barry Sanders with his mother, father, and his five sisters.

# Small Back, Big Plays

**B**arry's high school football coach took one look at him and thought he was too small to be a running back. But his father believed Barry could play and asked the coach to put him in the lineup. The coach agreed, and as a junior Barry played receiver and returned kicks.

Barry started his senior season as a receiver because his coach didn't like the way he ran side-to-side to elude defenders. He wanted him to run straight ahead.

In the fourth game, Barry finally began to play tailback. He quickly showed that was the position for him. The first game he started he ran for 274 yards and scored four touchdowns!

The 5-foot-8, 170-pound phenom averaged 10.3 yards per carry and six touchdowns a game. He rushed for 1,417 yards.

Although he was a great runner, Barry didn't feel pressure to succeed at football. "My pressure was to make up my bed, don't hit my sisters and 'C'mon boy, let's go work on this roof,' " Barry said.

Although he had a spectacular season, many colleges didn't even think about offering him a scholarship because of his size. Barry received only two scholarship offers, from Oklahoma State and Wichita State. Barry chose Oklahoma State.

"It's amazing to me how much attention coaches and scouts pay to size," Barry said. "I think that's where a lot of them fail. The fact that most of the big schools ignored me gave me incentive to show that it's not all about size."

Barry Sanders studying at Oklahoma State University.

# Humble Heisman Hero

*B*arry played little during his first two seasons at Oklahoma State.  He backed up Thurman Thomas, who later starred with the Buffalo Bills.

Barry didn't complain. He worked out in the weight room, adding 20 pounds to his impressive physique. He could squat lift 556 pounds, bench press 350 pounds, and jump 41 inches high!

But Barry didn't spend all of his time in the weight room. He also studied, taking classes in accounting, economics, and statistics as he worked on a degree in business management.

"I know I have an opportunity to be a positive influence on young people," Barry said. "I have never used drugs.  I try to study and stay out of trouble."

Barry took advantage of the playing time he had.  On his first kickoff return of the 1987 season, he caught the ball at the goal line, juked around defenders, and ran 100 yards for a touchdown.

The next season Barry repeated his incredible performance. He was the first player in NCAA football history to return the season-opening kickoff for a touchdown two years in a row!

"He just takes your breath away," Oklahoma State coach Pat Jones said.

When the Cowboys played Texas Tech in the Tokyo Dome in Japan, Barry showed how exciting the American game of football can be.

While Barry was in Japan he learned he won the Heisman Trophy, given to the best college football player. He accepted it reluctantly.

"It's just not that big a deal for me," Barry said. "And it's not really fair to so many other people. People take sports way too seriously. To some of them sports is a god, which is wrong."

The Cowboys earned a trip to the Holiday Bowl in San Diego. Barry rushed for 222 yards and scored five touchdowns as the Cowboys trounced Wyoming 62-14, finishing the season 10-2.

Barry could have broken the Holiday Bowl rushing record. But he chose to sit out late in the game to give others a chance to play.

During his junior year, Barry set 13 NCAA records. Among the many records that still stand are his 2,628 rushing yards, 39 touchdowns, and 234 points.

After the season Barry entered the NFL draft because he knew it would help his family financially when he signed a professional football contract.

"I just wanted to relieve some of those pressures," he said.

Oklahoma State tailback Barry Sanders, 1988 Heisman Trophy winner.

# A Young Lion

As the 1989 NFL draft drew closer, the Detroit Lions had a familiar question: Was Barry big enough?

As soon as Coach Wayne Fontes saw Barry run the 40-yard dash in 4.39 seconds and jump more than 41 inches into the air, he didn't wonder any longer.

The Lions chose Barry with the third pick of the draft and he signed a five-year, multi-million-dollar contract. One of the first things Barry did was write a check to Paradise Baptist Church in Wichita for $200,000.

Barry quickly proved himself on the football field. The first time his hands touched the ball, on September 10, against the Phoenix Cardinals, he ran for 18 yards.

Veteran players couldn't believe what they saw that season.

"You have to tackle him with good technique," Chicago's great middle linebacker Mike Singletary said. "If you try to blast him, chances are he'll spin out of it and you'll end up looking a little silly."

Sanders was so slippery some players accused him of covering himself with something slick. But game officials found nothing.

"I remember bracing myself to hit him. I knew I had him," Bears defensive end Trace Armstrong said. "He just stopped and turned and he was gone. He's like a little sports car. He can stop on a dime and go zero to 60 in seconds."

Even Walter Payton, the NFL's all-time rushing leader, was impressed. "I don't know if I was ever that good," Payton said.

Barry did so well that near the end of the Lions' final game of the season the team learned Barry was only 10 yards behind Christian Okoye of Kansas City for the rushing title. The Lions were leading Atlanta 31-24, and there was just enough time for Barry to have a few more carries and a shot at the title.

"Do you want to go in?" Fontes asked Barry.

"Coach, give the ball to Tony (Paige, a fullback)," Barry said. "Let's win it and go home."

"When everyone is out for statistics—you know, individual fulfillment, that's when trouble starts," Barry said after the game.

Even though he was modest, the awards came his way. He was named Rookie of the Year and was chosen for the Pro Bowl.

Barry Sanders carries the ball before making a touchdown in
the first quarter against the Chicago Bears.

# The Eyes Have It

*B*arry ran away with the rushing title in 1990, his second season, gaining 1,304 yards. He was named to the Pro Bowl that year, and in the next seven seasons.

The Lions won the NFC Central Division title in 1991 and beat Dallas in their first playoff game. But the Lions lost to Washington, the eventual Super Bowl champion, in the NFC Championship Game. Barry took the loss in stride.

"If I played all those years and didn't get a (Super Bowl championship) ring, I would definitely feel like I've missed out on something," Barry said. "But that's one of those unfortunate things that happen in this game. You can play for many years and it's not going to promise you anything."

In 1993, Barry became the Lions' all-time leading rusher with 5,674 yards, breaking Billy Sims' record. What made Barry stand out from the other running backs in the league? Barry thought it might be his eyes, which get big just before he starts to run.

"Your eyes aren't going to lie to you," Sanders said.

"You always get a feel for how people are playing defensively," he said. "Obviously, if they're pursuing hard, then there are going to be more cutback lanes. You have to see it and react to what you see."

Barry Sanders (20) races down the sideline for an 80-yard touchdown against the Indianapolis Colts.

# Barry's the Best

When the Lions met the Cowboys for a Monday night game in September 1994, everyone was wondering which running back would have a better game, Barry or the Cowboys' star runner Emmitt Smith.

Barry carried the ball 40 times for 194 yards, and the Lions won 20-17 in overtime. He did better than Smith, but didn't brag.

"There is not much to say about it," Barry said after the game. "The Dallas Cowboys defense is tough enough. Emmitt Smith was the least of my concerns Monday night."

Barry had an incredible season. He spun a New England defender around three times on his way to a touchdown, and had an 85-yard run with one shoe off against Tampa Bay. He set a Lions record with 237 yards against the Buccaneers. His rushing total was 1,883 yards, then the fourth-highest total in NFL history!

"You don't stop him," Vincent Brown of the Patriots said. "The only thing you can hope to do is contain him, hem him in. Every time he has the ball, he presents a problem."

Barry likes playing against tough defenders. It gives him an extra boost of energy, and makes him try that much harder and run even faster.

"For the most part, I just go out and try to get the most out of my runs and be as sharp as possible," Barry said. "All the hype and publicity going on prior to the game...is done away with in my mind. In this business there are so many other things going on that you just have to go out and do your job."

**Detroit Lions running back Barry Sanders takes time to sign autographs for waiting fans outside the Lions training facility at Saginaw Valley State University.**

# A Mover and a Shaker

**M**any running backs have short careers. Their performance declines quickly because of the pounding hits their bodies take. But not Barry. He has averaged five yards per carry in his career, one of the best marks in NFL history.

"I try to be consistent," Barry said. "I expect so much from myself, as much as any fan or any coach. There are a lot of distractions. Also, a sense of complacency can set in. A lot of things can happen. I try not to let anything keep me from being consistent."

Against the Packers in 1996, Barry showed he hadn't lost a step. He took the ball at the 15-yard-line on a third-down play. Barry was hit by Packers safety Eugene Robinson, bounced off him, and cut across the field. He faced seven defenders, eluding all of them on his way to the end zone.

That season he set the NFL record for most consecutive 1,000-yard seasons with eight.

"He's Houdini," Seattle defensive end Michael Sinclair said after the Lions beat the Seahawks 17-16 in November 1996.

In the last game of the season, a Monday Night contest at San Francisco, Barry needed 161 yards to win the rushing title. He gained 175, finishing the year with 1,553 yards, the second highest total in his career.

"He's like liquid out there, finds every crack, every opening," linebacker Broderick Thomas said. "He flows to daylight.  It's like tackling no other runner in the entire league."

**Barry Sanders (20) looks for running room.**

# Rushing into the Record Book

*B*arry got off to a slow start in 1997. The Lions had a new coach, Bobby Ross, and a new system. Barry rushed for only 53 yards in the first two games. Then he caught fire and rushed for more than 100 yards in each of the next 14 games!

Barry rushed for 2,053 yards and broke his own consecutive 1,000-yard season record, increasing his string to nine. In addition to sharing the MVP Award and winning numerous NFL player of the year awards, he passed Marcus Allen, Franco Harris, Jim Brown, Tony Dorsett, and Eric Dickerson on the all-time rushing list.

"If you add everything up, Barry Sanders is the running back who is Mr. Everything," Earl Campbell, the former Houston Oilers all-pro running back, said.

Miami coach Jimmy Johnson said he considers Barry the greatest running back ever. Despite Barry's success, his father contends

Jim Brown, who retired three years before Barry was born, is the best running back in NFL history. And Barry doesn't argue with his father.

"Jim Brown was probably one of the most dominating people on this field," Sanders said.

Barry Sanders joins the 2,000-yard club against the New York Jets in the fourth quarter at the Silverdome on Sunday, Dec. 21, 1997.

# A Lion with a Quiet Roar

You might not notice Barry Sanders if you saw him at a mall. He slips through crowds just like he slides past defensive linemen.

"I can move in a crowd virtually unnoticed, which is the way I like it," Sanders says, adding that it's helped his career.

"It's easy to be preoccupied with other things as you move higher in this game," he said. "That's one of the biggest reasons people decline. If I continue to love the game and work out the way I do, my decline will be more gradual than some other players."

He does not have a glamorous lifestyle. He drives a fancy sports car, a Jaguar, but it's more than 10 years old!

"When the football season is over, I just like to go back to my old neighborhood and play indoor or outdoor basketball," he said. "On the court, I like to shoot the jumper, and I especially like to play defense."

Barry doesn't think he's better than anyone else. When he was in London he was waiting to get into a trendy restaurant. He could have skipped to the front of the line, but he waited his turn.

"He's so humble and mild-mannered," said teammate Kevin Glover. "He never seeks glory."

Despite his awesome ability, Barry does not talk trash. He has never spiked the ball after a touchdown. He doesn't dance in the end zone.

"Usually guys will say to me before a game, 'If you score, you've got to spike or dance,' " Barry said.

"Sometimes I think about it, but when I actually do score, either I'm tired and just want to get back to the bench, or it just doesn't cross my mind."

Barry won't brag about his accomplishments, but he's happy with his football career and his life. "I am definitely content with the way things have gone for me in and out of football," he said. "For the most part I wouldn't trade it for anyone else's experience."

Even after many seasons in the league, Barry still gets nervous and excited before a game. "I'll be anxious. I'll be on the first bus to the stadium. I'll sit in the locker room with butterflies," he said. "I'll be excited. It still matters to me. A lot."

**Barry Sanders, center, is congratulated by his father, William, left, and teammate Ryan Stewart, right, after Barry rushed for 2,000 yards in a season.**

# Barry's Stats

## Profile

Height: 5 feet, 8 inches

Weight: 200

Born: July 16, 1968

College: Oklahoma State

Position: Running back

## Awards

1988 Heisman Trophy

All-time NCAA single-season leader in rushing (2,628 yards), scoring (234 points) and TDs (39)

Rookie of the Year (1989)

NFL rushing title (1990, 1994, 1996, 1997)

NFL Player of the Year (1991, 1994, 1997)

NFC MVP (1994, 1997)

NFL co-MVP (1997)

First player to rush for 1,500 yards in three consecutive seasons (He has four heading into the 1998 season)

First player to rush for 1,000 yards in eight consecutive seasons (He has nine heading into the 1998 season)

Named Pro Bowl starter in nine consecutive seasons

All-Pro (1989, 1990, 1991, 1994, 1995, 1996, 1997)

All-Pro second team (1992)

Associated Press Offensive Player of the Year (1994, 1997)

## *Barry Sanders' Season-by-Season Rushing Totals*

| 1989 | 1,470 yards |
|------|-------------|
| 1990 | 1,304 yards |
| 1991 | 1,548 yards |
| 1992 | 1,352 yards |
| 1993 | 1,115 yards |
| 1994 | 1,883 yards |
| 1995 | 1,500 yards |
| 1996 | 1,553 yards |
| 1997 | 2,053 yards |

## *2,000-YARD RUSHERS*

| Eric Dickerson | 1984 | 2,105 yards |
|----------------|------|-------------|
| **Barry Sanders** | **1997** | **2,053 yards** |
| O.J. Simpson | 1973 | 2,003 yards |

# Chronology

**1968** - Barry Sanders was born on July 16 in Wichita, Kansas, the seventh of 11 children of William and Shirley Sanders.

**1985** - As a senior, he began playing tailback for the North High School football team. Gained 1,417 yards rushing.

**1986** - Began his freshman year at Oklahoma State University. He played very little his first two seasons.

**1988** - Broke or tied 24 National Collegiate Athletic Association records and won the Heisman Trophy.

**1989** - Drafted by the Detroit Lions, the third pick of the first round. Set a Lions single-season and rookie record, gaining 1,470 yards. Chosen Rookie of the Year and selected for his first of nine Pro Bowls.

**1990** - Won NFL rushing title with 1,304 yards.

**1991** - Led NFL with 17 touchdowns.

**1992** - Became first player to gain more than 1,500 total yards in each of his first four seasons. Set Lions all-time rushing record, with 5,674 yards, breaking Billy Sims' record.

**1993** - Injured his knee and missed last five games of the regular season. Returned for playoffs and gained 169 yards against the Packers.

**1994** - Rushed for league-leading 1,883 yards, then the fourth-highest total in NFL history.

**1995** - Rushed for 1,500 yards and caught a career-high 48 passes for 398 yards.

**1996** - Won third career rushing title with 1,553 yards.

**1997** - Rushed for 2,053 yards, the second-highest total in NFL history. Gained 100 or more yards in a record 14 consecutive games.

# *Glossary*

**DRAFT** - National Football League's method of allowing teams to choose players, usually from college teams.

**FIRST DOWN** - The first of four chances the offense has to gain 10 yards or cross the goal line.

**HEISMAN TROPHY** - Awarded each year to the best college football player in America.

**MVP** - Most Valuable Player. The MVP Award is given to the top player in the NFL each season.

**OPENING KICKOFF** - Ball kicked to start the game.

**PLAYOFFS** - Postseason games played by division winners and wild-card teams.

**RECEIVER** - A player on offense designated to catch a pass.

**RUNNING BACK** - Offensive player who lines up behind the quarterback and usually runs with the ball.

**RUSHING** - Running with the football.

**TAILBACK** - Offensive player who lines up farthest behind the line of scrimmage and carries the ball on most running plays.

**TOUCHDOWN** - A score worth six points. A team must cross the goal line in the other team's end zone to score a touchdown.

# *Index*